GOVERNOR

In the Company of
ANN W. RICHARDS
Governor of Texas

Written and photographed by

RICHARD SOBOL

Foreword by Ann W. Richards

Government in Action Series
COBBLEHILL BOOKS
Dutton/New York

For Ronnie Mae

Library of Congress Cataloging-in-Publication Data

Sobol, Richard.
    Governor : in the company of Ann W. Richards, Governor of Texas /
written and photographed by Richard Sobol.
        p.   cm.
    ISBN 0-525-65194-2
    1. Governors—Texas—Juvenile literature. 2. Richards, Ann, date—
Juvenile literature. [1. Richards, Ann, date–   2. Governors.] I. Title.
JK4851.S62   1994   353.976403′13—dc20   93-40426 CIP AC

Published in the United States by Cobblehill Books,
an affiliate of Dutton Children's Books,
a division of Penguin Books USA Inc.,
375 Hudson Street, New York, New York 10014

Designed by Charlotte Staub
Printed in Hong Kong   First Edition
10 9 8 7 6 5 4 3 2 1

FOREWORD

I grew up in a small town in Texas during the Depression. My daddy worked driving a delivery truck for Southwestern Drug Company and my mama kept a garden where she grew everything we ate. My parents never wanted me to have to work as hard as they did, but that was all I ever saw them do. The message I got was that the only things of any real value in life were family and hard work.

I remember listening to my daddy tell stories that would make us laugh, and I remember how we would huddle around the radio and listen to President Roosevelt. His strong voice gave us a sense of optimism and purpose, and when he talked it seemed like he was talking just to you. He gave us all such hope, and he taught us that we could solve our problems if we worked together.

I never dreamed back in Lakeview that one day I would be the Governor of Texas. I only knew that if I worked hard like my parents taught me, good things would come my way—and they did.

As Governor of Texas, I have had the privilege of meeting thousands of good people who work hard and who care about making this world better for our children. I have met schoolteachers who cherish their students' future, doctors who care for their patients like family, and public officials who understand the profound responsibility of government is to *serve*.

Growing up in Lakeview, it was easy to see what truly matters. Now that I have children and grandchildren, it is important to me to act on that understanding—to build a government that means something good in people's lives and to build a society where our children know they can be anything they want to be. That's what I learned listening to the radio, and that's what I want you to learn from this book of photographs—that you have leaders who believe in you and, by working together, we can build a nation where our opportunities are boundless and where dreams really do come true.

Ann Richards

In July, 1992, I was hired as the official photographer for the Democratic National Convention in New York City as Bill Clinton and Al Gore were nominated to be the Democratic party candidates for President and Vice President. This allowed me special access to roam the podium where I could get close-up photographs of all the important people who were attending and speaking. Governor Ann Richards was the Chairperson of the convention and our paths kept crossing on the crowded stage. As Chairperson, she spoke frequently from the podium and at one point, when she needed to address the convention, I accidentally blocked her path. I felt terrible about this and after her speech was finished I attempted to apologize for getting in her way. She stopped me in midsentence and said, *"Now,*

Ann Richards as Chairperson of the Democratic National Convention.

Honey. Don't you worry about it. If I couldn't get around someone like you on my own, I wouldn't be where I am today. You just go ahead and do your job as best you know how." "Whew," I gasped to myself and thought—what a remarkable person. I sure would like to get to know her better. As the idea for this book was developing, she was the obvious first choice.

Ten months after our collision in New York, I found myself in Austin, Texas . . . in the company of Governor Ann Richards.

A Governor is for many people the only visible symbol that they have of their state government. The work of thousands of individuals who help to build roads, teach in schools, prepare meals for the elderly, take care of the sick, and protect the natural environment may all come to be represented by the public image of the Governor. This is a huge responsibility for one person. And an awful lot of work. Constant hard work. A Governor is always on the telephone or at a meeting, jumping from one issue to the next. Balancing insurance regulations and school finances, highway construction and flood controls in a turning kaleidoscope of activities.

Officially the job of a Governor involves preparing a budget to control the spending and finances of the state, influencing the process by which new laws are written, and directing the work of dozens of state agencies. Beyond this already full agenda come thousands of special requests from elected officials and private citizens, all of

Ann Richards in front of the State Capitol in Austin.

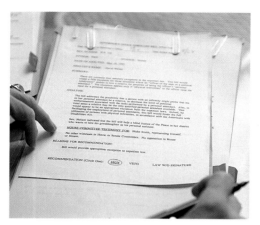

Sample piece of legislation.   *Signature.*

which must be addressed, pulling minutes and hours from a Governor's crowded schedule.

"There is never a letup in this job. There is never a point when you are not 'The Governor.' You are on call twenty-four hours a day as everyone's Governor . . . It is relentless. I have done other work in my life that was also hard, but it really didn't mean anything when it was finished. With this job, you work hard, but when it is over, you feel like you have made a difference."

For Texas Governor Ann Richards, the day starts quietly enough in her private apartment in the Governor's Mansion with a quick read-through of the morning newspapers—accompanied by the first of many cups of coffee. Next she looks through the stack of folders left by her staff, each color-coded to separate the bills that need her signature from the letters that need responses, the legal cases to review, and the invitations to consider. By 7:00 A.M., the phone calls begin as her life is shared with those who need her help or opinion. Her day starts to spin like a merry-go-round. Her path through the day will cross the lives of thousands of people and her decisions will

At home in the early morning. ▶

affect even more. She will be thrown into the center of conflicts and be asked to perform more than a few minor miracles. Late in the evening she will return home to the Governor's Mansion to face an additional hour or two of paperwork. This routine will be repeated at least six days each week and often seven. And yet, there is no one that she would trade places with.

"I learned more about politics from running a household than I have from any single occupation. Managing a household, providing care and encouragement for children, is a hard, hard job. Raising children prepares one for negotiating and working with large numbers of people. Like most families, we had our share of arguments at the dinner table. Loud ones, too. But they all have to get resolved. No one can leave the table angry. Disagreements have to be settled so that everyone gets to have a piece of the pie, everybody has to have an opportunity to save face. That is a lot of what I have to do in this job. In fact, that's the hardest part of my job, but it is also the most rewarding."

Ann Richards likes a relaxed atmosphere.

Governor Richards and her staff share a group of offices at the Texas State Capitol complex in Austin. The offices are designed for function—simple, clean, and orderly. Nothing plush or fancy, except for the walls, which explode with bright displays of contemporary art. This is a reflection of the political personality of Ann Richards, functional and orderly, yet able to break the ice at a serious meeting with a joke that knocks people off their straight-back chairs.

"You bet being funny helps accomplish things. I've always maintained that people don't realize how many brain cells it takes to be funny. And politics ought to be fun—after baseball it is our next favorite national pastime."

The atmosphere around the executive office is usually friendly and relaxed. The Governor's office door is almost always kept open and members of her staff are encouraged to pop in and share their ideas or suggestions. To help relieve the stress that comes along with the important issues that they deal with each day, there is a lot of laughter and friendly kidding around. A few times a day the Governor herself can be found leaning on an office doorway, sharing a new joke or reviewing a movie. There are some times, though, when the tension in the air is so highly charged that each footstep on the soft carpet seems to echo from wall to wall. Staff people tiptoe around, moving in slow motion. Even the telephones and fax machines somehow seem to know to respect the silence and they appear not to interrupt at these moments.

Most of her office work ends up being done in ten-minute blocks of time, if she is lucky, before the phone rings or someone pokes his head through her open office door. Those few times each day when the door is closed are signals to the staff that some trouble is brewing. Ann Richards is not a person who keeps many secrets. She

Working with her staff.

shares much with her staff and when a meeting or phone conversation is made behind closed doors, the staff gears up to help work out the problems that may be developing inside the office.

She is always asking questions—seeking guidance and willingly listening to arguments made against a decision and openly speaking up when she does not agree with someone. In the end, though, the responsibility for each and every decision rests with her alone.

Inside her office the Governor is on the phone trying to hammer out an agreement to control the cost of insurance. Her patience has run out. She feels the people of Texas are being squeezed by a group of unfeeling businesses. She wants results and straight answers. No political niceties are left in this battle. No more talk around the edges of the issues. The difficult battles are the ones that inspired her to run for Governor in the first place. On this one she won't back away. The anger in her voice is obvious as she speaks into the phone.

"Don't tell me what this fight is about. I know what the fight is about! What can we do to solve this? How can we get moving? The insurance board is supposed to look after the interests of the people, not work for the insurance companies. The people of Texas pay for this insurance board and if you forget who you are working for, then we are just wasting our money. I will have no choice other than to eliminate the board and your job will go right along with it. Am I clear on that? I need an answer by tomorrow. You call me, I'll be here."

Hanging up the phone, she takes a long, deep breath, before glancing down at her daily schedule. In two minutes she is due at a lunch reception for visiting concert pianist and old friend, Van Cliburn. A quick sip on her ever-present cup of coffee and up she goes, striding out the door all full of smiles. Changing gears as easily as a bicycle on a steep hill, she puts the harshness of the last few minutes behind her.

"In preparation for a job like this, people have to have a solid core, a center that is connected with the people that they are there to serve. Some people in government can forget very quickly. I can stay in this office for several days without seeing people, real people, and my whole outlook changes. A week when I am trapped in this office, in this building, this isn't real. When I go down to south Texas or to east Texas, I can go into a cafe where people are drinking coffee, talking about their lives, or when I walk down Main Street, now that's real. I was down in south Texas, in a small town, not long ago and these people came running out and said, 'Please,

Ann Richards likes to be accessible to the people of Texas.

With Van Cliburn.

could I come visit around the back?' There was a woman who had kidney failure and other medical problems. They told me that she would be so thrilled if I would come and see her. So we walked around behind what was, to put it mildly, a very modest house, paint peeling everywhere, to a place in the back that didn't have but two rooms, two tiny rooms. This woman was in this bed, and next to her were bunk beds. I knew that two children slept there, right next to her. She was very, very sick, and she probably didn't have very long to live. She told me how she couldn't get anyone to come and help her with her kidney dialysis treatments. Now, these bills and votes on health care and insurance take on a very different meaning when you have sat in the bedroom with a woman like that. They are not just words on paper anymore. I'll never forget her."

The three-minute walk from the Governor's office to the reception for Van Cliburn at the Capitol becomes a half-hour series of thirty-foot, slow-motion surges forward, punctuated by handshakes, waves, smiles, updates on legislation, questions about how votes are going, details filled in about all sorts of issues. Housing. Insurance. Farming. Mexico. Education. Endless questions. "Did you get the letter about this, or the one about that . . ." As she moves slowly forward, weaving and bobbing through a knot of bodies, faces light up as she turns each corner. Her hair, the color of radioactive snow, shines out against her brightly colored jacket. She is hard to miss. Nobody can just pass by. Everybody wants a piece of her. When she stops for someone, for that moment, she is there only for them, listening and responding. During this walk, she will stop and hug a state senator whom she is fighting on a bill and pose for a picture with the daughter of a state representative who constantly votes against her. However strongly she fights for what she thinks is right, she also respects those who disagree with her and remembers that

Her walk from the office to Senate floor is a series of stops.

14

those are political disagreements. There is no room in her life to let politics get in the way of personal friendship. She is the Governor of all of Texas, those who vote for her as well as those who vote against her.

This routine of work will continue throughout her four-year term. In November, 1994, she will be up for re-election again. She will present herself before the voters of Texas and they will judge her. They will look at the job that she has done and they will decide if she gets to serve another four years as Governor.

Governing a state as large as Texas is a unique challenge. At least six or seven times each month, Ann Richards will climb aboard the eight-seat plane that the state of Texas provides for her and attend

On the airplane.

Talking with a group of fifth and sixth graders.

town meetings, dedications, forums, school visits, and government programs far removed from her office in Austin. This is a necessity in a state which covers 266,807 square miles. Some weeks she may fly more than two thousand miles to keep up with events within the broad borders of the state. Her plane becomes a traveling office, a place to have a private meeting or review the text for an upcoming speech during the long hours of travel. It also allows her to keep up with other important people who may be visiting Texas, like Janet Reno, Attorney General for the United States, who came to Sweetwater to dedicate a museum for the women pilots of World War II or Henry Cisneros, U.S. Secretary of Housing and Urban Development, who came home to San Antonio for his daughter's high school graduation.

With Janet Reno in Sweetwater.

With Henry Cisneros, San Antonio; with Lady Bird Johnson at formal dinner.

"It is important for people to know that their government is accessible. That I am accessible. I hate the business of having government removed from people. They need to see us, they need to talk to us. I try to be out as much as I can. I think that meeting and touching people is a way for them to know that government is not just a big impersonal bureaucracy. It's not just big fat reports and numbers on a page. The Governor, the person who runs it and is head of it, understands that it affects the lives of human beings. I am glad that people can come up to me at the grocery store or at a restaurant or movie theater. If people want to have a picture made with me or if they want to tell me something, that's great. Lots of times people stop me and it's just personal stuff. It doesn't have anything to do with government. I think that people think of me as their friend, and I'm happy with that."

Her sense of caring and compassion comes from deep within. She is most often dealing with programs that affect the lives of thousands of people, but the individuals around her are still important. Even a Governor can take a few moments to ask for the results of a Little League game or check up on weekend plans. Leaving her Capitol office for a television interview, she noticed that the suit jacket of Chuck McDonald, one of her press staff, had a rip in it. *"Stop right here, Chuck,"* she commanded. *"You can't be looking all ragged today. Not with me anyhow."* And ignoring the giggles of those passing by, she pulled a safety pin out of her purse to do a quick repair. *"There, now you are almost a gentleman,"* she said as they proceeded toward the hot glare of the TV lights, laughing together.

Television has become an important tool for elected officials today and Ann Richards understands this well. She knows that for many Texans television will be the only place that they will meet. No matter how much she travels around the state or how many people stop by her office in the Capitol, most people will only get to know

A quick repair to Chuck McDonald's coat.

her through the glowing rectangles of a television broadcast.

Preparing video greetings and messages that will be aired in local communities is one of the ways that she stays in touch with many of the small towns in Texas. For this video taping she sits alone in the center of an ornate room filled with echoes of Texas history. As she quietly reviews her thoughts to herself, the cameraman gently interrupts to say, "Ready to start any time, Governor." As if waking from a nap, her head lifts up, her eyes sparkle like exploding fireworks, and her smile grows round and wide like a fresh-cut slice of watermelon. She speaks directly into the camera, eyes bright and words full of energy, using phrases that are deeply personal, speaking of her pride for a high school class that did well on its test scores and asking for volunteers for a state agency looking to recruit compan-

Ann Richards at videotaping.

ions for older people who live alone. Not exactly a script that would win any Oscar nominations, yet when she finishes, the lighting and sound crews break into a loud round of applause.

"*I like setting the tone, I like giving an image to the state. I think that that may be difficult to describe, but that means people having a good feeling about Texas. I like it that the people inside Texas feel good about themselves. That they have a sense of hope and self-confidence. Especially the schoolchildren. I like the idea that the children feel that their government is a friendly place.*"

Thousands of school groups visit the State Capitol each year and Governor Richards seems as excited to run across them as they are to see her in person. Walking over to the State Legislature, she is all smiles and high fives as she accidentally runs into a group of schoolchildren visiting the State House building. Eagerly grabbing their hands and putting her arms around their shoulders, she starts a rapid dialogue with them:

"What do you like best in school?

"Did you tour the Governor's Mansion?

"That's your house, you know. I am just lucky to be living there now.

"Who do I work for? Who owns this State House?

"Now think about it. . . . When you buy something at the toy store you have to pay a sales tax on it, don't you? That means that you are a taxpayer just like your parents are. So you help pay my salary. I work for you.

"You are the owners of this building."

High fives with a group of schoolchildren.

As the kids swarm around her and wave pens and papers for her autograph, her staff gently reminds her that others are awaiting her at a hearing to discuss state funding for schools.

"I am sorry, kids, but there are so many of you and only one of me. If I started signing these, I guess I would be here until midnight and never get this old government working today."

All of the walking around the State Capitol to meetings, receptions, and press interviews probably adds up to a two- or three-mile aerobic workout each day. It also helps to keep the Governor in circulation with reporters and state legislators. As she passes back and forth through her staff offices she often pops in to check out what is happening, asking, *"How are we doing? Anything I need to know?"* When she returns once again to her own office it usually is to find a small mountain of phone messages that she must plow through. As lunchtime passes by unnoticed, a staff member waits for a quiet mo-

On the floor of the State Legislature.

22

ment to ask the Governor if she would be interested in a grilled chicken sandwich. Her reply—*"James, I am so hungry now that you could be offering me roofing tiles with hot gravy and I'd be happy to eat them."*—brings a wave of laughter to her office staff.

With a half dozen people working on the details of the daily schedule, the Governor has most of her time planned out for her weeks in advance. Her schedulers guard her time as if it were gold. One of the few people who can ignore the professional staff members and stomp all over this process is her five-year-old granddaughter, Lilly Anna. When it is time for her all-important graduation from kindergarten she goes right to the top, the Governor herself, whom she calls Mammie, and asks her to come, with only a few days' notice before the celebration. The response is pure grandmother. A warm hug and "of course." The Governor/grandmother will take her only break from the pressure of the final week of the Texas State

Staff luncheon.

*At granddaughter
Lilly's graduation.*

Legislative session, where important laws are being debated, to be with her granddaughter and her classmates. It will be up to the staff to quickly remake the schedule to fit this in. When graduation day comes, the Governor will be there. The class shares its delight and the children crowd around to have their pictures taken with Lilly's grandmother, taking turns wearing the paper graduation cap that their teacher has made for them.

"I have had Lilly's class over to visit at the mansion and she knows that her grandmother is a Governor. I am just not sure that she doesn't think that everybody's grandmother is a Governor!"

Ann Richards remembers that despite the long hours and pressures of being Governor, she still must find time to stay in close touch with her family and friends. Some weeks her only breaks from work will be to invite her children and four grandchildren over for a picnic or a barbeque. She may have only a half hour free between a meeting and a formal dinner, but she will try to relax by taking in a game of croquet together in the grass or picking vegetables in the gardens of her home.

Sometimes, late at night, she will sneak away to a movie, looking for escape in a darkened theater for two hours. Away from staff, away from phones, away from papers needing her signature, and away from questions which only she can answer, she will lose herself

With grandchildren at the Governor's Mansion.

in the story moving across the screen. Munching slowly from a giant bucket of popcorn resting on her lap, here she can relax totally. If there were to be a real emergency her security agent, sitting quietly a few rows behind her with a two-way radio connected to his ear, would be able to alert her. It would take a BIG deal to interrupt a movie, though. To Ann Richards these few private hours are precious. For the rest of each day, each week, and each month, the people and problems of the state of Texas are in her mind at all times. That's what it means to be Governor.

Relaxing at a movie.

Getting to Know Ann Richards

What do you like to do for fun?
Walk on the beach, go fishing, see movies.

What relaxes you the most?
Reading and playing with my grandchildren.

What do you like to do best at home?
Sleep.

What is your favorite junk food?
Peanut M&M's and fried chicken.

How do you maintain your weight?
I buy larger sizes.

What are your favorite things to spend money on?
Books, gifts for friends.

What do you miss now that you can't do because you are Governor?
Driving my own car.

What don't you miss?
Looking for a parking space.

What do your grandchildren call you?
Mammie.

What are your favorite movies?

Aladdin, Beauty and the Beast *(with my grandchildren)*, The Firm.

Who are your favorite movie stars?

Robin Williams, Susan Sarandon, Dolly Parton.

What music do you listen to?

All kinds, especially Lyle Lovett and Willie Nelson.

What are your favorite books?

The Secret Garden, The Firm.

Who are your best friends?

My children.

How did your hair turn gray?

Have you met my children?

When you were a kid did you want to grow up to be Governor?

Back when dinosaurs roamed the earth and I was young, politics was a male province. Women made the coffee and men made the decisions. No more. We have changed that.

What would you like to do next?

Being Governor is the best job in the world. I am happy right now.

MORE FACTS ABOUT THE GOVERNOR

5,000 bills and constitutional amendments are filed in each legislative session, which occurs once every two years
- 1,000 bills are passed and cross the Governor's desk for action
- 900 are signed into law
- 34 are vetoed (Governor has the power to cancel them if they do not have a two-thirds majority vote supporting them.)
- 66 become law without the Governor signing

Governor receives between 7,000 and 10,000 pieces of mail each week
- includes 1,200–1,500 requests for visits, only a few of which she will be able to attend
- each piece of mail is answered

Governor travels at least 1,500 miles per week throughout Texas
- gives 3–4 major speeches and 4–5 brief remarks per week
- 40–50 school visits per year
- 25 meetings in office per week

50–100 people stop by office each day to say hello, leave information, or ask for an appointment with the Governor or staff member

- 232 people work directly for the Governor
- 110 people are appointed by her and work in other agencies

Governor's office includes the following sections:
- executive, correspondence, press, schedule, legislative, budget, planning, policy council, accounting, computer services, constituent service, personnel, legal counsel, energy, film and music, mansion

Total budget: $223,328,872.00
- $205 million of this money passes through the Governor's office for program funding and operating grants for ongoing projects

Governor's office gives out gifts to visiting dignitaries, politicians, and school groups each month, including:
- 1,000 pencils
- 1,000 bookmarks
- 5 silver or glass bowls
- 5,000 official signing pens per legislative session

Executive office goes through 25 packets of coffee each week
Governor snacks on 5 home-baked cookies each afternoon

ACKNOWLEDGMENTS

The staff of Ann Richards welcomed me to Texas and gave me assistance and guidance throughout this project. Thanks to Bill Cryer, Kirk Adams, Bill Ramsey, Joy Anderson, Margaret Justus, James Mathis, Gabby Garcia, Virginia Lisnow, David Miller, Cecile Richards, Janet Allen Shapiro, Krystal Duncan, Pat Cole, Leticia Vasquez, Don Temples, and the Texas Department of Protective Services Governor's Detail.

Special thanks to Chuck McDonald who carried the ball (and occasionally my camera bags) to arrange for me to observe the life of the Governor and watched over me on a daily basis.

Thanks also to Ginny Terzano and Ron Brown who brought me to the Democratic National Convention, worked me twenty hours a day, and introduced me to Ann Richards.

For their support and help in reviewing the text, I thank my friends Joshua Rubenstein, Betty and Art Bardige, Rick Friedman, Sharon Grollman, David Thurston, Catharine Hayden, Rosanne Lauer, Romando Fufanellow. And Richard Moover for the fine Tex-Mex, and Steve Brettler who has always been there with equipment, but returned again with something even more valuable.

A thank-you is not nearly sufficient to cover the courtesies and graciousness that were extended to me by Ann Richards herself. She taught me what a "Texas-size welcome" means as she kept me by her side in her office, car, plane, and home. I am honored to have shared her companionship.